LEAD YOUR FAMILY

Twelve ready-to-use ideas to spiritually lead your family

Brian Jennings

International Standard Book Number 978-0-89900-555-3

Table of Contents

Anytime

Foreword

A popular game we sometimes play at our house is called JENGA. If you're not familiar with it, it's a game that begins with a tall stack of blocks and then each player removes the blocks one by one until the tower of remaining blocks comes crashing down. The person who pulls out the last block loses. So all you can do is lose. I suppose it's not a very uplifting game for kids, but hopefully that means it's building character. At least that's what we tell ourselves. Anyway, I want you to imagine a tower of stacked JENGA blocks in front of you. Each block is important because each block adds strength and stability to the tower. With each block that is removed the tower becomes more unstable until eventually it collapses.

In Brian's book, "Lead Your Family," he gives us one building block after another to help us build a strong tower. As I read this book, I found a number of the suggestions gave me a block for a space in my tower where a block was missing. This book is filled with simple and practical blocks that you can start to build with right now that will strengthen the home God has entrusted you to build.

In grade school Brian Jennings and I regularly sat next to each other in children's church and sang a song based on a story that Jesus tells at the end of the Sermon on the Mount. The story is known as "The Wise and Foolish Builder." (If you see Brian, I'm sure he would be glad to sing a verse or two for you.) In the story we read of two builders—one builder builds his house on the rock and the other builder builds his house on the sand. Both houses face a terrible storm. The rains come down, the streams rise, and the winds blow and beat against the two houses. The house built on the sand falls with a great crash, but the house on rock stands firm.

As parents we are all building a house, and every house will face its share of storms. It all comes down to the foundation. But here's the thing about foundations—they tend to get overlooked. If you go to someone's beautiful new house you might compliment their decorative flair, their color choices, the architectural uniqueness; but what you don't do is walk into the house and say, "nice foundation." But the truth is, it doesn't matter how impressive the house is if it's built on a bad foundation. As parents let's not get so caught up in the business of our homes that we overlook the foundation. Accept the challenge to "Lead Your Family" and begin building a strong foundation today.

Kyle Idleman
Teaching pastor at
Southeast Christian Church
and author of
Not a Fan, *AHA*,
Gods at War, and *H$_2$O*
2015

# Introduction

If God guaranteed that your kids and grandkids would faithfully walk with Him in exchange for your right leg, you'd probably order crutches. You care deeply and passionately about the spiritual health of your family. In your moments of greatest clarity, it dominates your dreams. But caring about your family's spiritual health and actually leading them towards spiritual health are two different things.

Life wars against your ability and commitment to spiritually lead your family.

Busyness wars against you.

Frustration wars against you.

Stress wars against you.

Self-doubt wars against you.

Laziness wars against you.

Past failure wars against you.

Reasons to disengage from spiritually leading your family abound. But take heart—you stand in the company of the overwhelmed. We can all identify. Even the seemingly picture-perfect family is not doing as hot as they appear.

If you feel inadequate, don't sweat it. Attempting to spiritually lead your family does not require great faith in yourself. It requires great faith in God. Take a deep breath, exhale, and admit that you aren't good enough to do this on your own. You'll need God to hold your hand.

God commissioned you to lead your family. Yes, your church will help your child grow. Yes, camps and retreats will help your child grow. But you are the primary influencer. And if God has commanded this, He'll provide you with all you need. **God will give you everything you need in order to spiritually lead your family.**

You'll face obstacles, but the wonderful news is that God created your children as spiritual beings. He has set eternity in their hearts (Ecclesiastes 3:11). He has hardwired their hearts to search for meaning, purpose, hope, and love. He's hardwired their hearts to search for Him. You have probably already noticed that they have a spiritual nature and a longing for God. This reality breathes hope into our souls.

The purpose of this book is to provide you with twelve ready-to-use ideas to help you spiritually lead your family. Some ideas may fit best during a specific season of your calendar, but all of them can be implemented quite quickly. Each chapter can be read in less than ten minutes, but the power is in the application. I encourage you to read a chapter, and then discern if or when you will put it into action. And be ready for God to give you an idea that will work much better for your family than the ones I've listed below.

Okay. Let's get to it!

Chapter 1
Make a Family Commitment

The following ideas will flow more smoothly if your family stands on common ground. If you're married, ask your spouse to partner with you in this journey.

While you don't need your kids' permission to proceed (you should proceed, regardless), getting their buy-in will benefit everyone. So pursue their blessing and commitment to helping your family spiritually grow. I packaged my encouragement to you into a devotion—a short Bible study which you can use to raise the bar of spiritual pursuit in your family.

Find a time when you can have the attention of your family for about 15 minutes. For those of us with big families, this requires some work. Ask everyone to put down basketballs, toys, and books. Turn off the TV. Silence the phones.

Review and feel free to edit what I've written below, so that it comes genuinely from you. And include your kids by having them read some verses if you think that will engage them.

Commitment Devotion

Hey, family, we have something really important for you to hear. Please give us your best attention and participation for about 15 minutes. Please. It's so crucial.

In Deuteronomy 6, God teaches the Israelites how to live. This chapter specifically speaks to families. And it still applies to us today. So hear these words from God to us.

Read Deuteronomy 6:1-3.

Our greatest desire in life for you is that you will walk with the Lord. Parents shared this same desire thousands of years ago, too. God commanded us (your parents) to spiritually lead our family. Here's how:

1. Parents spiritually lead by having a genuine love of God. (Read Dt. 6:4-6.)

We know we aren't perfect (Give an example.), but we commit to loving God with every fiber of our being.

Did this verse remind you of anything that Jesus said? When Jesus was asked what the greatest command was, He quoted this verse, so we see how important it is.

2. Parents spiritually lead by teaching their children every chance they get. (Read Dt. 6:7-9.)

We want to teach each other about God. We want to teach you, but we want you to teach us too. We are going to lead some family devotions, where we learn to love God more. We also want us to all be looking for times to talk about God, even as we go throughout our normal day.

3. Parents spiritually lead by being aware of false gods. (Read Dt. 6:13-14.)

We don't have the idols like the Israelites had. But do we still have idols in our world (things that we worship instead of God)?

Let's make a list of idols we see in our world.

Some people in our world have made sports, hobbies, money, jobs, popularity, and even family the number one priority in their lives, which means that they are worshiping these things. We want to make sure that God is our number one priority.

4. Parents spiritually lead by preparing to answer questions. (Read Dt. 6:20-25.)

I don't have all of the answers. I never will. But if I keep learning and growing, I'll be able to better lead you and others to know God. And if you commit to growing in the Lord, you'll be able to help others grow in the Lord, too.

We believe that God is the only hope for our world and for our family. He loved us so much that He created us, and then He even sent His Son to die for us, so that our sins could be forgiven and we could have eternal life with Him.

So, as a family, we desperately long for God. We need God's wisdom to instruct us. We want to pray. We want to influence others.

Will you make a commitment to grow with us?

(This might be a good time to talk about how you want to start having some devotions like this or regularly praying together, etc.)

Pray, asking God to help your family grow in Him.

During the School Year

Take advantage of a new semester by implementing some routines that will spiritually nourish your family.

Chapter 2
Routine & Reward

Mornings can be tough on any parent. Kids roll over when woken up, get dressed too slowly, play a game instead of gathering their homework, and make us tell them everything they need to do EVERY DAY. This gets tiring, especially when we are tired too.

Who should we blame for this early morning suffering? I'll give you a hint: we shouldn't blame the kids. It's the parents who foster this frustration.

My wife Beth and I decided that we desperately needed a new routine. We formed a plan and communicated it clearly to our kids.

At 6:45, we wake them up—and we make sure they are really awake. They are expected to get out of bed, get fully dressed (even shoes), comb their hair, go to the bathroom, get their things together, and be at the table by 7:05.   **19**

If they arrive late, they will be going to bed earlier that night. Rules without teeth are just optional suggestions.

If they are on time four days in a row, fully ready, not grouchy, and did not need to be awakened multiple times, I will take them to have donuts on Friday. (Thanks for this idea, Kathy Morton.) My kids love donuts, but maybe there is a better motivator for your kids.

The stinky part comes when one of them gets left out of donut day. But we have to stick with it.

The new routine may be difficult to establish at first, but consider the rewards. Your kids will learn some discipline (their days of needing to be somewhere on time are only beginning). They'll have time for physical and spiritual nourishment. And you'll gain peace and calm. Win, win, win!

In the next chapter, I'll tell you an even more important part of our mornings. It's what happens at 7:05.

Chapter 3
Fill Them Up

We know that our kids, in spite of a great school, will hear hurtful words, feel wounded, and be exposed to opinions that may or may not be true. And in all of this, they'll be tempted to think, say, and do things that will dishonor God.

What will guard their hearts? What will prompt them to care for the lonely kid on the playground? What will guide them to answer the teacher truthfully, even if it will hurt their grade? What will help them discern what is true and right when their friends choose poorly?

Beth and I can help them, but they need more. They need God's Word in their hearts and His Spirit in their lives.

We feed our kids breakfast, not only to build a healthy habit, but so they won't crash halfway through the morning. Honeycomb cereal may not be the breakfast of champions, but it powers their little bodies through the morning.

If we prioritize feeding their bodies, should we not also feed their heart, soul, and mind?

At 7:05, if they haven't eaten yet, they get their breakfast, I sit down at the table with them, and we read a small section from the Bible or a brief family devotion. We talk about it and then pray for our family, our concerns, and our world.

As I write this, we are reading about ten verses a day from the book of James. I ask them a few questions about it. Sometimes I also challenge them to memorize a verse or more that week, and I include a financial incentive.

James has been a great book for us to read because it tells us to "persevere," to be "quick to listen, slow to speak and slow to become angry," and to "not show favoritism." It's loaded with application for our family.

Our devotions aren't fancy. Flies on the wall aren't impressed at all. Sometimes it doesn't go very well. Sometimes I'm rushed. Sometimes a kid spills an entire water bottle on my Bible (well, that only happened once). But this time in God's word is crucial, and we're going to stick with it.

Chapter 4

Napkin Notes

I estimate that I ate about 1,864 sack lunches during my school years (usually a peanut butter and jelly sandwich). Sometimes as I was surveying the contents of my lunch, a big smile would spread across my face. My friends would notice, and they would make me show them my napkin.

My mom occasionally drew funny pictures on my napkin, and she'd tell me that she loved me. Lots of times she'd draw a basketball player making a shot, if I had a game that night. I loved those pictures. They reminded me of her love. Kids need that, you know. School can be a tough place.

I was thinking about this last week, so I decided to do the same thing for my kids. I am artistically challenged, but I gave it my best shot. It took me ten minutes to complete two drawings. Beth did the other one, and it was significantly prettier.

I encourage you to do this for your kids. If they buy their lunch, slip a note in their backpack or find another way to be creative. Write a prayer, a silly joke, or a favorite verse. Remind them of your love and God's love. They may or may not act excited, but trust me—they love it and need it.

Summertime

Summer offers great opportunities for families, but it can also lead to lots of frustration. Plus, it goes by so fast that I am afraid to blink. I deplore feeling like we did not get the most out of a summer. We decided to implement a couple of habits/rules in our house unique from our school-year routines. Our goal was to establish some routines that would promote peace, creativity, and spiritual growth.

Chapter 5
Slay Electronic Addictions

Summer Rule #1: Thou shall not play or view any electronic devices before lunch.

When your kids hear the rule, they won't dance for glee or write songs in your honor. But hear me out.

The average teenager spends more than seven hours a day looking at a computer or cell phone.[1] This activity (or lack thereof) decreases physical, relational, and emotional health. This phenomenon threatens spiritual health too.

I don't need to convince you that many kids and adults are consumed by computers, phones, video

---

[1] Multiple studies agree on this number, including research completed by the Kaiser Family Foundation (kff.org/other/poll-finding/report-generation-M2-media-in-the-lives/).

games, and all manner of electronic devices. You know it. You see it. Let's call it what it is: addiction. Yes, technology can be a beautiful thing for us all, but only when managed wisely.

I also probably don't have to convince you that electronics tend to infect your kids with jealousy, complaints, and moodiness. Do you ever feel like you should gear up with a referee shirt and whistle when the computers and video games light up? When our kids start arguing about whose turn it is to play, my wife wants to drive far away. Very far.

We noticed that if our kids spent the first three hours of their day in complete slothfulness, they'd spend the rest of the day loafing around and complaining of boredom. It's a real joy to have four zombies meandering around the house doing this.

So we enforced the "no electronics until after lunch" rule. Once they've eaten their lunch, completed their Bible reading (more on this in the next chapter), made their bed, and gotten dressed, they are welcome to play an hour of electronics that afternoon. Any sibling-spats about electronics will jeopardize this freedom.

Gone are the morning arguments about playing time. Instead, our kids busy themselves by reading, drawing, shooting hoops, journaling, or swinging in the backyard. It forces them to be creative.

Oh, and if any of the kids utters the unspeakable phrase, "I'm bored," they won't be bored for long. They'll be assigned additional chores. (Admit it, this sounds fun to enforce.)

We love the rule. My wife does not have to referee four children's electronics time in the morning, it helps us proactively protect them from unhealthy addictions, and it helps their minds grow.

Try it. Give it some time. I think you'll love it. And eventually, your kids will accept it as normal.

Chapter 6
Read, Write, Review

Summer Rule #2: We shall individually read one section of the Bible in the morning, write down a few notes, and then discuss it with the whole family in the evening.

I took the time to explain to my kids why we were doing this, and I made it clear that they had no other option (so they may as well get on board). And I also reminded them of all the fun stuff they'd get to be doing this summer. We held firm, and they quickly adapted. In fact, they all are actually enjoying the new routine quite a bit. This shouldn't surprise us if we believe that God's Word is precious and good.

When they eat breakfast, or right after they finish, they read one chapter from the Bible (which we've communicated). They also open up a notebook and write something down about the chapter. We grant lots of freedom here. They can write their favorite verse and explain why, they can write a question they have from the text, or they can tell how the text applies to their life. My goal is for them to think more deeply as they read.

Looking for insight spurs us to read more attentively. Our family discussions at night have demonstrated our increased level of learning. A few weeks ago, as we were sharing what we'd written, we discovered that all of us had written down the same verse from Hebrews 3: "Let us fix our thoughts on Jesus. . . ." My oldest asked if it was possible to think about God while focused on a task. It led to a vibrant discussion about doing everything to honor Christ. The kids began thinking about how they could do this through their daily activities. In that moment, God's Word became very real to us.

My kids remind me if we forget to discuss the Scriptures in the evening. I like that a lot. Summer schedules get hectic, but we've done our best to do this when we are home.

Now, Beth and I enjoy our quiet morning times on the back patio, and a kid or two usually joins us. I pray that these habits stick for them. I pray they'll stick for your family too.

All the Time

All the Time

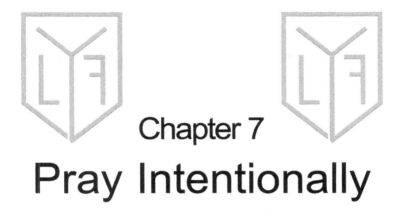

Chapter 7
Pray Intentionally

Maybe your family already prays. Great! The next step is to pray intentionally.

We have to ask this question, "What does God care about most?" As we study Scripture, we read of His unending desire to draw all people to Him. We see of His great concern for the vulnerable, the oppressed, and the hurting. We are convicted by His calls for holiness, unity, maturity, and growth.

Then we must ask, "Do I pray about the things that most matter to God?"

Should we pray for the sick? Absolutely.

Should we pray before we eat? Yes.

Should we pray for safe trips and a good night of sleep? You bet.

But we should pray for so much more than these things. Our prayers should predominately be about the things on the top of God's priority list. In doing this, we share God's perspective of human events, we engage in the spiritual battle, we position ourselves to be used by Him, and we teach our kids what to value most.

Pray for the Kingdom to grow. This means praying for your unchurched neighbor, the missionaries your church supports, and people groups who've never heard the gospel.

Pray for the vulnerable. In our home, we pray for Blackbox International,[2] which helps trafficked boys. We pray for Daima, the girl we sponsor through Compassion International. We lift up our friends serving on the mission field. My kids don't fully understand all of these things yet, but they will. When my son saved allowance and birthday money in order to give $50 to Blackbox, I nearly wept with joy.

Pray for inward transformation. As you read through the Bible, this will give you plenty of ideas. Pray for things like love, patience, and joy. God's not done with us yet.

Pray for any cares and concerns. Teach your family that your first response to any problem or crisis is to pray.

---

[2] I serve on the board and absolutely love this organization. See http://blackboxinternational.org.

Pray for each other. Pray not only for your present, but also for your future. Pray for God to prepare your children for adulthood. Pray for who they will become.[3]

As a family, consider starting a prayer journal. Once in a while, I have all of the kids write a full prayer that day. It's awesome to see them engage this way. Writing helps us formulate our thoughts into intimate prayers.

Pray, pray, pray.

---

[3] See Appendix 1 for an example from my friend, Gincy Hartin, of what to pray for your kids.

Chapter 8

Schedule One-on-One Time

My ten-year-old boy's birthday present included a St. Louis Cardinals game with me on the way to a convention. It was just the two of us for four days. He'd been counting down the days, and when it finally came, he ate up every second of it.

On the second day, as we walked through a long hallway with our arms around each other, he said, "Dad, I have to keep reminding myself that this is not a dream." Once again I was reminded of the value of one-on-one time.

Carving out one-on-one time with our kids is a high priority that so quickly slips away from us. Our schedule manages us, instead of the other way around. Weeks turn into months if we don't put ink on our calendar, so we must be proactive.

One-on-one time rarely includes a big trip (although it's awesome when it does). Small dates to get a snow cone or go on a bike ride are the norm.

While scheduling times is the best, we also look for impromptu times to do this. I look for times that I can sneak away from work a few minutes early, or even take one of my kids with me to run some errands. I've noticed that if I offer to take one of them with me, they are apt to go. If I offer to take all of them, they'd rather clip their fingernails or something. An errand may not be fun, but one-on-one time is always valuable.

Our kids can be somewhat defined by their situation and their siblings. That's a reflection of their reality, but I want to make sure they know Beth and I are available, we care, and we are pouring our lives into them as individuals, not just a collection of kids. If you have several kids like us, you know what I'm trying to say here.

This week I took one of our boys out for a hamburger and shake. Before I picked him up, I wrote out ten reasons why I love him. I could see his spirits soar during our quick meal. It was the highlight of my week, and I think of his too. I never cease to be amazed at how different our kids can be when we have them one on one (and it's all good).

A few weeks ago during an ice cream date, Beth learned that one of our kids was carrying a wound from unkind words said months ago by a friend at school. Feeling the safety and affection of the moment, our child chose to share about the incident. Removed from the noise of three other children, Beth was able to give the best of her attention.

Lastly, I encourage you to give each child your full attention, if even for a few minutes, once they are in bed. Kiss them, pray with them, and listen.

Anytime

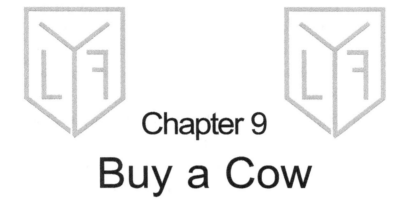

Chapter 9

Buy a Cow

You might think it strange that a family with no land, barn, hay, ranching skills, or experience in the dairy industry would purchase a cow. We thought it was one of the best decisions we made in The Year: The Year of the Cow.

One summer, our church encouraged people to take a faith challenge. We handed out sealed envelopes, each containing a challenge that was doable but a faith-stretch. If a person chose to open the envelope, they committed to keeping the challenge.[4] We told people they could modify it, if that would make it more effective.

Beth's challenge involved feeding the hungry, so she chose to buy a cow. We knew that we'd never pet the cow, but a family in an impoverished country would.

---

[4] We got this idea from Christ in Youth, who does this at their summer "Move Conference" for high school students. Check out http://ciy.com

One cow can dramatically change, if not save, the lives of an entire family. We committed to saving $500 in order to buy it. The organization we chose would do the footwork. They'd get the cow to the family and teach them how to care for it. The family would be able to drink its milk (one cow can provide 120,000 cups of milk in a lifetime), sell the extra milk, and have lots of fertilizer. The family can also sell or give away offspring of the cow to another family in need. It's a beautiful thing.

Our challenge was to figure out how to save $500. At the time, we budgeted $120 a week on grocery items for our family of six (which included some food and items for our baby). We usually eat out at least once a week as a family ($25–35), and Beth and I each buy a couple of lunches during the week (about $20).

We committed to not eating out for several weeks, as well as slashing our grocery bill. By the way, we talked to our kids about this, explaining that we wanted to love people like Jesus did. We told them that we could make a difference, but it would require their sacrifice. They wholeheartedly supported our adventure.

Week 1: Other than baby items, we purchased no new items. We lived off the fat of our pantry for that entire week. It was amazing what we found in there. We ate some unusual concoctions, but we survived.

Week 2: We only bought milk, fruit, beans, rice, and stuff for PBJ sandwiches. Not needing to buy our normal groceries for two weeks saved us about $175. Not eating out brought our total to $285.

We offered a challenge for others to partner with us. Four families committed to join us in our cause. One friend gave up Starbucks coffee for several weeks. One family sacrificed eating out. Another sacrificed two weeks of any entertainment that would cost money. They all generously donated, not knowing what the others would give. And when we added it all up, we celebrated. The tally at the bottom of our notebook was almost exactly $500. Perfect!

Our family learned valuable lessons:

1. We should quit whining about food. We were so thankful for anything other than rice or peanut butter after two weeks. But even more valuable than this, we developed gratitude for having our stomachs filled.

2. Simple foods can sustain us. While we welcomed different foods after two weeks, we also acknowledged that we

could survive with a very simple diet. Millions of people do just that.

3. A healthy mindset views food primarily as fuel for the body (sustenance), rather than indulgence. We thank God for the yummy food He gives us. We enjoy the creativity of a skilled cook. Enjoying food is great, but this should not replace the primary purpose of food.

4. We have *extra*, and it's fun and good to give our *extra* to those who don't have *enough*.

5. We really like rice, beans, and bananas. We learned this Brazilian recipe from a friend. It cost us $4 to feed the whole family this meal. We still eat it often.

6. We give because God has given to us. We kept reminding ourselves of this biblical principle.

In the end, we sacrificed very little. And if we do it again, we'll probably keep it a secret. But we wanted to encourage you to develop a family plan to give in a special way. We don't care if anyone copies our model, but we hope and pray that you will do something. It might teach you lessons that you'll never forget. You might not buy a cow, but you will be moooooved.

This much I know, it is more blessed to give than to receive (Acts 20:35).

Chapter 10

Take the Acts Assessment

I love that we learn the practices of the infant church. Following the first ever "Christian sermon," three thousand people were baptized, and Acts 2:42-47 tells us what they did.[5]

> They devoted themselves to the apostles' teaching and to fellowship, to the breaking of bread and to prayer. Everyone was filled with awe at the many wonders and signs performed by the apostles. All the believers were together and had everything in common. They sold property and possessions to give to anyone who had need. Every day they continued to meet together in the temple courts. They broke bread in their homes and ate together with glad and sincere hearts, praising God and enjoying

---

[5] New International Version

the favor of all the people. And the Lord added to their number day by day those who were being saved.

A healthy family looks like a healthy church. Both require healthy leadership. While the following exercise would be healthy for a church, consider if the following are true of your family:

They devoted themselves to the apostles' teaching.

Are you leading your family to be devoted to Bible study and teaching? Church leaders and teachers can help, but you must own this responsibility. Regardless of your understanding of Scripture, you can take small steps today in order to know God better and equip yourself to teach your family. You and your family can follow the example of Jesus.

"And Jesus grew in wisdom and stature, and in favor with God and man" (Luke 2:52).

They devoted themselves to fellowship.

Biblical fellowship includes but extends well beyond a mere gathering. The early church committed to take care of each other. Some would have lost jobs and families as a result of following Christ. The church took care of their needs, even selling possessions and land. Sacrifice fosters genuine, deep fellowship.

Are you quick to sacrifice in order to care for your family? Does your family sacrifice for others in need? Does your family support your church? Does your family share a sense of purpose and joy?

They devoted themselves to the breaking of bread.

They honored the Lord's Supper (communion). Do you follow this practice that Christ initiated? Some of the most meaningful times of communion for me were when my family honored this practice while on a trip. It reinforced our family's commitment to Christ. It taught me that we were committed to Christ, regardless of where we were. Does your family honor holy practices that draw you to Jesus?

They devoted themselves to prayer.

You cannot look anywhere in Acts without seeing that prayer was not just part of their life—it was their life. Is your family dependent upon God through prayer? Do you give thanks to blessings? Do you lift up concerns? Is prayer your first move?

Healthy churches and healthy families draw people to the Father. You may not need to add on a bedroom, but if your family models the joy, sacrifice, prayer, purpose, and gratitude of the early church, your spiritual family will grow.

Take a week to honestly evaluate your family. Look for areas to improve or change. The Lord will go with you. Take the Acts Assessment.

Chapter 11
Evaluate Your Sports and Hobbies

Note: This chapter deals with sports, but the principles can be applied to any hobby or activity. If necessary, take the short, mental leap, and apply it to your family's life.

The Beauty of Sports

As the third base coach for my son's tee ball team, my job was to instruct kids to halt at second, come to third or dash home. This was a great job, even though many of the kids viewed my instructions as mere suggestions.

I remember a time when a player rounded second and I waved him to third and then home. A few moments later, the coach in our dugout asked me where this boy was. We looked up and he was back on first. He had rounded all of the bases, including home, and gone back to first.

By far, the best part of coaching third base was that I had the very best view of the players rounding second base, grinning from ear to ear as they ran. I've loved coaching and I've also loved playing.

I still get goose bumps from remembering the thrill of winning for the first time as an underdog. I was in junior high, we were playing a team that had beat us by thirty-nine points the year before; they had not lost in three years, and they had guys with beards. I think some of their players had been in eighth grade for a long time. Their small town packed the tiny gym, but they went home stunned. We pulled off the improbable upset. We could have run home without touching our feet to the ground.

One of the beauties of sports is that the effort and passion in a tiny community gym can rival what you'll find in Boston Garden or Yankee Stadium.

Sports and hobbies are a beautiful gift from God. They bring rest to our minds, they brighten difficult days, they foster discipline and commitment, they form friendships, and they promote physical health. Sports and hobbies are a beautiful gift to us.

The Ugly of Sports

But sports can have an ugly side, too. I read of a father who slipped drowsiness-inducing drugs into the water bottles of his son's tennis opponents. His conniving act was discovered only after one opponent died from the medication. The father was sent to prison for eight years.

Consider the difference between the boy running, grinning from ear to ear, and the obsessed father spiking kids' water bottles. What went wrong? Erik Thoennes describes these two opposing views:

> One has preserved within sport the healthy, joyful expression of the deep human inclination to play, the other has locked into a utilitarian understanding of sport that squelches play and the perspective-giving power of sport. One appreciates the actual process of playing a sport; the other has sadly turned sport into an ugly expression of human pride, insecurity, envy and malice. What will keep us from turning sport into something ugly [idolatry] rather than beautiful?[6]

---

[6] http://projecthopespeaks.org/wp-content/uploads/2012/04/Created-to-Play-Chapter-Thoennes.pdf

Perhaps you feel like "idolatry" is too strong a word. But when you consider how much time, money, and passion we give to sports, it's not a stretch. David Platt appropriately mocks the worship of sports (specifically, college football which dominates his hometown) in a hilarious, yet depressing, portion of a sermon.[7] People talk about the game all week, spend thousands to watch it, call the field "hallowed ground," stand for three hours and scream at the top of their lungs for their team. They empty their wallets, overwhelm their calendars, and consume their thoughts with sports.

Unhealthy devotion to sports isn't confined to large-scale events. Youth sports require more and more time, money, and commitment than ever. Parents feel the pressure to give their kid every advantage, which may mean yearlong participation. For many families, sports dominate long seasons of their lives.

I've gathered principles regarding this topic from Scripture, personal experiences, and wise thinkers. Below each principle, you'll find one or more action steps your family can take in order to align yourselves with the principle.

Principle 1: "Participation in sports must be informed by the knowledge of God."[8]

---

[7] You can watch the video here: https://www.youtube.com/watch?v=Ve9jPfJeT2k.

[8] From David Platt's excellent sermon on August 17, 2013, https://itunes.apple.com/us/podcast/brook-hills-audio/id319699838?mt=2#.

When we behold the glory of God, it makes all of the difference. When we cast our glance away from God's glory, we lose perspective. How foolish to think that a silly game played by twenty-year-old kids, whom we'll never meet, actually matters. We may begin to even worship such things.

Let it not be. Refocus. Fix your eyes on Jesus. Order all things under the umbrella of God's glory.

> So whether you eat or drink or whatever you do, do it all for the glory of God. Do not cause anyone to stumble, whether Jews, Greeks or the church of God—even as I try to please everyone in every way. For I am not seeking my own good but the good of many, so that they may be saved (1 Corinthians 10:31-33).

> ➢ **Action: Commit to growing in your knowledge and love of God, as an individual, a family, and as part of the local church.**

As you daily dwell on God, His Word, and His concerns, you'll gain perspective. You may need to revamp your calendar. You may need to build new routines. Do whatever it takes.

> ➢ **Action: Be humble.**

God's glory, goodness, holiness, power, and love drive us to our knees. We aren't worthy, yet He showers us with grace.

C.J. Mahaney writes, "Only an ignorant, arrogant fool would draw attention to himself and exalt himself in light of the glory of God."[9] There's no room for personal adoration and self-promotion in the Kingdom. I'm not the King, so I'll posture myself as the servant, thankful to be called *son*.

Principle 2: Sports are a good gift. We can praise God for them, or we can replace God with them.

"Every good and perfect gift is from above" (James 1:17). We don't help ourselves by stating that sports are evil. God has given us a beautiful gift.

Platt points out that the book of Romans teaches that sin is often not bad things; sin is often a good thing that we begin to treasure more than we treasure God. Sin twists the good into evil. Sin replaces the Giver with the gift.

Don't let the gift become greater than the Giver.

➤ **Action: Be thankful to the Giver.**

If you enjoy sports, be thankful to the Giver. Praise Him. Adore Him. Remember that the gift (sports) never deserves our praise.

Begin praising God in the morning. Make a list, praising Him for whom He is and for what He's done.

---

[9] C.J. Mahaney, *Don't Waste Your Sports,* Crossway, 2010.

Principle 3: All things must be done to bring glory to God.

There are no exceptions to the command. ALL things. It's a great command, because sports make lousy gods. Any god other than The God leaves us empty and headed on a path of destruction.

Perhaps you've never considered that you can bring glory to God with sports. But think of the testimony of a player who chooses integrity over winning, the coach who uses sports as a platform for meaningful friendships, and the family whose church allegiance causes them to sacrifice some "great opportunities."

Whether you are a player, parent, or fan, you can honor God with your decisions about sports.

➤ **Action: Examine your life.**

Examine your heart. Is your heart devoted to sports?

Examine your mind. Tim Keller says, "The true god of your heart is what your mind automatically, consistently goes to when there is nothing else to think about."[10] Do sports dominate your thoughts?

Examine your conversations. What do you most passionately speak about?

[10] http://www.christianitytoday.com/ct/2009/octoberweb-only/142-21.0.html?paging=off.

Examine your emotions. Are you inordinately happy or sad based on the outcome of a game? What do you really care about? What would others say?

Examine your use of money. How much money do you pay in a year to participate in or watch sports?

Examine your calendar. How much time did you give to sports this week? This month? This year? How much time did you give to God? Family? Serving?

> **Action: Be a missionary.**

John Frame writes, "In one sense of course, we cannot increase God's glory. But when we speak truly of Him and obey His Word, we enhance His reputation on earth, and we ourselves become part of the created light by which people come to know God's presence. So Jesus says that His disciples are 'the light of the world' (Matt 5:14), as He is (John 8:12; cf Matt. 4:14-16)."[11]

The bleachers, dance studio, and ball field serve as our mission field. Nothing has brought more joy to our family's life than seeing God work through us to draw others to Him.

[11] John Frame, *The Doctrine of God*, P & R Publishing, 2003.

Before we sign-up a child for any activity, we talk about the real reason we play. We play to bring glory to God, which means that we're missionaries. And before we get out of the car or leave the house, on our good days, we pray that we'll be a light to others. We've missed chances. I've blown opportunities. But we'll keep at it and we'll celebrate that even losses on the field can end with victories in the home.

➤ **Action: Model godly behavior when you play, watch, and cheer.**

"Do everything without complaining or arguing" (Philippians 2:14). There God goes again. He has the audacity to grant zero loopholes. So we must not complain even when the referee blows the call, or when the coach unfairly benches our kid.

If you dismiss this command, you'll blackout the light that God intends to shine through you. If you argue and complain, you'll teach your children how to respond to authority, so don't be surprised when they respond this way to you.

Sports can be a beautiful gift to your family. They can also be a destructive idol. Choose to honor God with your sports.

Discussion questions for your family:

- What have been the most God-honoring by-products of sports and hobbies for our family?

- What have been the most negative?
- Is there a sport or hobby that we need to adjust? Is there one that we need to completely drop?
- Do we need to make changes or limitations to our schedule and budget regarding sports and hobbies?
- Have we transferred a love for God and our church to an allegiance to a sport or hobby?
- How can we become missionaries through sports? (Get practical.)

Additional Resources:

Intentional Walk features the stories of Adam Wainwright, David Freese, Lance Berkman, Matt Holliday, Carlos Beltran, Jason Motte, Mike Matheny, and other members of the 2012 St. Louis Cardinals, written as those players and the rest of the team tried to repeat the 2011 world championship. The book talks about how they became Christians and offers their testimony about what it means for them to have God play such a prominent role in their lives.

Created to Play: Thoughts on Play, Sport and the Christian Life is a paper written by Eric Thoennes, professor of Biblical and Theological studies at Biola University.

http://projecthopespeaks.org/wp-content/uploads/2012/04/Created-to-Play-Chapter-Thoennes.pdf

I devoted an entire sermon to this topic. It adds some depth and passion to this chapter.[12]

Chapter 12

Prepare for the Baptism Question

If you are studying Scripture and seeing examples from church, your kids will naturally ask about baptism. It is not unusual for a parent to ask me for advice about their child's desire to commit to Christ. But when my son began asking me about baptism a few years ago, I had a chance to walk in the shoes of those parents, instead of just the minister.

Spiritually leading our children is the greatest of all privileges, but that doesn't make it easy. If you embrace the biblical concept that we all must choose Christ for ourselves, then you recognize that there are times when a child is not ready to be baptized. On the other hand, we do not want to squelch the genuine desire of a mature child longing for Christ. None of us will ever have complete understanding of salvation (at least in this life), but how can we figure out if a child at least has enough understanding to make this commitment?

Questions to ask before your child is baptized:

1. Have they studied intently? Encouraging your children to study on their own (along with learning in special classes or church settings) is a great step. You should be studying, too, but allow them the responsibility to study some on their own. For a simple, biblical study of baptism, go to http://www.brianjenningsblog.com/baptism.

2. Do they feel guilt from sin and love for God? Motives matter. Kids may want to be baptized because they saw a friend receive attention, they desire to please their parents, or maybe they just really want to take communion. Obviously, these are not the motives they need. My experience teaches me that if a person does not understand that we are covered in guilt, they are not to a necessary place of understanding. If we do not understand our guilt, we do not appropriately grasp God's grace and love.

3. Are they persistent? Time allows us to test a child's sincerity. It's not the only test, but

it's an important one for children. If your child mentions baptism once, but never mentions it again, that should tell you something.

4. Are they mature enough with their cognitive abilities? My four-year-old is a great joy in my life, but she is not capable of a sincere, lifelong commitment to Christ. If she was baptized this week, 15 years from now, she will probably have zero memory of her choice, and she will deeply doubt her commitment. And she may, like many adults I counsel, be a bit resentful of her parents who encouraged/allowed her to do something that she was not ready to do. Abstract reasoning is needed here. While each child is different, this ability usually begins to develop around third grade. Parents need to discern when this ability has developed enough to proceed. (Note: if your child has grown up in church, he or she will be able to give all the right answers long before they develop enough mature thinking to make this commitment. A wise parent understands this.)

5. Have you received input from godly leaders? It saddens me when parents do not

ask for any sort of guidance and help with this huge decision. Ultimately, they are the spiritual leaders in their home, but I find it unwise not to seek prayer and wisdom from those who may have helpful and experienced input.

As with the rest of parenting, these decisions may not be cut and dry. But if you are wrestling with it, that encourages me. That means you are praying, seeking wisdom, and treating your child's spiritual health with great care.

I'm thankful that we serve a God of grace. We will not always navigate these decisions perfectly (for ourselves or our children), so we'll lean on grace and keep seeking truth.

(Thank you, Rose Ann Dunson, who has been faithfully leading the Children's Ministry of Highland Park Christian Church for 20 years, for your help with this chapter.)

Closing Notes

Being obedient in spiritually leading your family does not guarantee that they will spiritually grow. God lets us all choose. Some things are out of our control. But God calls us to obedience, and then we pray for the obedience of our children too.

Most parents I speak to feel overwhelmed. That's okay. When you became a parent, you signed up to feel overwhelmed. Be thankful for God's grace and provision. He'll take you as you are and lead you. He'll give you people to help you. And if you let Him lead you, you'll find yourself with everything you need to do the great work that only you can do.

Please, my dear friends, spiritually lead your family.

Appendix 1

"Eight Things I Pray for My Daughters"

(by Gincy Hartin)

Gincy Hartin is a good friend who serves at the First Christian Church in Chicago. He has a couple of daughters, just like me. He graciously allowed me to share eight things that he prays for his daughters:

1. I want them to show love, mercy, and kindness to all people without partiality, prejudice, or hypocrisy.
2. I want them to be humble learners.
3. I want them to grow up to be people of influence in the world, to be the kind of people that others love to be around, to be positive people

(not whiners and complainers), and to be encouragers who lift others up instead of bringing them down.

4. I want them to be generous with their time, money, and talents, because they are genuinely concerned about others.

5. I want them to know that they are capable of leading in our church, nation, and world.

6. I want them to find their ultimate sense of self-worth, not in a relationship with a man, but in a relationship with Jesus Christ.

7. I want them to know what it really means to love and be loved by God, and to love and be loved by others.

8. I want them to be bold and courageous, living lives that are guided by their faith rather than fear, and to be confident when facing the challenges that life will present.

About the Author

Brian and his wife, Beth, live in Tulsa, Oklahoma, with their four children. He'd gladly regale you with stories of the time they adopted, gave birth, and waded through a significant job transition within the span of four months.

Brian has served at Highland Park Christian Church ever since graduating with a Bachelors of Theology from Ozark Christian College in 1998. He also serves on the Board of Trustees for *Blackbox International*, which provides care for boys who are victims of sex trafficking.

Brian enjoys long dates with Beth, writing, tennis, family bicycle rides, and outhustling young guys on the basketball court. You can read his blog at brianjenningsblog.com.

Find information and resources about this book, as well as blog posts with more ideas and helps for your family at **www.leadyourfamily.net**.

Acknowledgements

Beth, my love, my best friend, my partner, I'm blessed beyond measure to share this journey with you. Thanks for encouraging me to write. Thanks for upping my game.

Cole, Levi, Shurabe and Hope, I often find myself missing you by about 10:00 in the morning, just a few hours after I drop you off at school. I pray that you will change the world for the glory of God.

Mom, Dad, Charles, and Nanci, I could never repay the gift that you gave us: God-honoring homes full of joy, love, and security. But I'll try.

Highland Park Christian Church, you've never made me choose between my family and you. Instead, you've loved my family as your own. Family is what we are.